A Kid's Guide to Drawing the Countries of the World™

How to Draw
Peru's
Sights and Symbols

Cindy Fazzi

The Rosen Publishing Group's
PowerKids Press™
New York

In loving memory of my father Hernando Melliza

Published in 2005 by The Rosen Publishing Group, Inc.
29 East 21st Street, New York, NY 10010

First Edition

Editor: Rachel O'Connor
Book Design: Kim Sonsky
Layout Design: Albert B. Hanner

Illustration Credits: Cover and inside by Michael Donellan; p. 18 Albert B. Hanner.

Photo Credits: Cover and title page (hand) by Arlan Dean; p. 5 © Jeremy Horner/Corbis; pp. 9, 38 © Wolfgang Kaehler; p. 10 © Stephanie Colasanti/Corbis; pp. 12, 13 photos by Alois Eichenlaub/Archivo Sonoviso, Cajarmarca from the collection of Camilo Blas. With permission of Andrés Zevallos.; p. 14 © RF/Geo Atlas; p. 16 © RF/Eye Wire; p. 20 © Marco Bleeker; p. 22 © Eric and David Hosking/Corbis; pp. 24, 42 © Kevin Schafer/Corbis; p. 26 © Charles & Josette Lenars/Corbis; p. 28 © Yann Artthus-Bertrand/Corbis; p. 30 Dave G. Houser/Corbis; p. 32 © Hulton-Deutsch Collection/Corbis; p. 34 © Charles & Josette Lenars/Corbis; p. 36 © MIT Collection/Corbis; p. 40 © Inga Spence/DDB Stock Photo.

Library of Congress Cataloging-in-Publication Data

Fazzi, Cindy.
How to draw Peru's sights and symbols / Cindy Fazzi.
    p. cm. — (A kid's guide to drawing the countries of the world)
Summary: Presents step-by-step directions for drawing the national flag, kantuta flower, Machu Picchu, and other sights and symbols of Peru.
Includes bibliographical references and index.
ISBN 1-4042-2740-7 (Library Binding)
1. Drawing—Technique—Juvenile literature. 2. Peru—In art—Juvenile literature. [1. Peru—In art. 2. Drawing—Technique.] I. Title. II. Series.

NC655.F378 2005
743'.89985—dc22

                    2003022080

Manufactured in the United States of America

CONTENTS

Let's Draw Peru

Historians believe that the people who first inhabited Peru, a country in South America, came from Asia. It is thought that they crossed the Bering Land Bridge from Asia into North America around 20,000 B.C. These first inhabitants then spread throughout North America and South America. Most likely, they were nomads who hunted animals and gathered plants for food. Around 2000 B.C., some of the Native Americans, or Indians, started farming. They settled along river valleys in the area that is now called Peru.

Around 900 B.C., a group of people called the Chavin lived in the northern mountains of Peru. The Chavin people created the first civilization in Peru. They shared the same culture, or way of life. Other civilizations followed the Chavin, including the Nazcas, the Moches, and the Chimu. In 1450, a small group called the Incas attacked the Chimu kingdom. This was the beginning of the Incan Empire.

In 1532, a group of Spaniards led by Francisco Pizarro arrived on Peru's northern coast in search of

From 1463 to 1493, the Incas expanded their territory. To the north, Incan lands reached all the way to the border of present-day Colombia and Ecuador. To the south, Incan territory reached as far as present-day Chile. This is one of the most rapid expansions in history. Pictured here are the Incan ruins of Machu Picchu.

gold and other riches. The Spaniards beat the Incan rulers and took over the empire. It was the beginning of 300 years of Spanish rule in Peru, during which time the Peruvians became poor. Indians and mestizos, those with mixed Indian and Spanish ancestry, had to work hard on farms and in mines to pay high taxes to the Spanish government. The Peruvians rebelled against Spain in 1780, but the rebellion was quickly stopped.

Other native peoples in Spanish colonies in South America also rebelled in the early 1800s. For example, General José de San Martín freed his country, Argentina, from Spanish rule. He also helped to free Chile. Next he went to Peru to help the people break away from Spain. San Martín announced Peru's independence on July 28, 1821, even though much of the country was still controlled by Spain. To complete Peru's separation from Spain, General Simon Bolívar of Venezuela led an attack against the Spaniards in Peru in 1823. The rebels finally beat the Spanish forces in 1826.

The military has traditionally played an important role in the Peruvian government, and many generals have served as president over the years. Peru has changed its constitution several times. The one in effect today was adopted in 1993. Under this constitution, the president is elected by the people to serve as head of state and government for five years. The people also elect a congress with 120 members to make the country's laws.

In this book you will learn more about Peru and how to draw some of the country's sights and symbols. Directions are under each step. New steps are shown in red. You will need the following supplies to draw Peru's sights and symbols:

- A sketch pad
- An eraser
- A number 2 pencil
- A pencil sharpener

These are some of the shapes and drawing terms you need to know to draw the Peru's sights and symbols:

— Horizontal line

◯ Oval

▭ Rectangle

 Shading

〜〜 Squiggly Line

▱ Trapezoid

△ Triangle

| Vertical line

〜 Wavy line

More About Peru

Peru has a population of 26.5 million people. About 6 million people live in Lima, the capital. About 46 percent of Peru's population are Indians and 43 percent are mestizos. The rest of the population are people of Spanish ancestry, blacks, and Asians. The official languages in Peru are Spanish and Quechua, the language of the Incas. Most Peruvians speak both. There are from 30 to 40 other dialects spoken throughout the country.

Peru does not have an official religion, but 97 percent of Peruvians belong to the Roman Catholic Church. Before Spaniards arrived in Peru, the Incas worshiped many gods and spirits. Viracocha, the creator of the Sun, the Moon, the Stars, and Earth, was the most important god to the Incas. After the Spaniards came in the 1500s, they introduced the Catholic faith in Peru.

The Spaniards who first traveled to Peru saw how rich the country was in natural resources, such as gold and silver. That is why there is a Spanish expression, *vale un Peru*, or "it is worth a Peru," which means

The Quechuan Indians are descendants of the Incas. They speak Quechua, the language of the Incas, and they still use many of the farming methods that were used by their Incan ancestors. Here a Quechuan Indian boy wears a colorfully beaded hat.

something is very precious. Today, however, Peru is one of the poorest countries in South America. Peru's economy depends a lot on farming, which does not bring in a lot of money. Many Peruvians own small farms that barely produce enough food for the farmers and their families. Others work on large cooperative farms. Workers on a cooperative farm own the farm as a group. Peru's major crops are coffee, cotton, sugarcane, potatoes, and bananas. Farmers also raise llamas and sheep for their wool and meat.

Peru is one of the world's main producers of zinc, copper, and silver. It also has oil, iron, and gold. It sells large amounts of guano, which is made mostly of bird droppings and is used as fertilizer. Peru's factories make chemicals, furniture, paper products, steel, and textiles. There are many small businesses that make and sell arts and crafts, such as pottery and handwoven cloths. The tourists who visit Peru's ancient ruins, desert, and jungle also bring in money. Every year, about 500,000 tourists travel to Peru.

Every June 24, the Indians celebrate their winter solstice. This is the shortest day of the year in the Southern Hemisphere. On this day, the Indians pray for the return of the Sun through dances, parades, and fires. They call this festival Inti Raymi, which means "Father Sun."

The Artist Camilo Blas

Camilo Blas was born in 1903 in Cajamarca in northern Peru. His uncle, Mario Urteaga, was also a famous painter. In the 1920s, Blas studied painting in the National School of Fine Arts in Lima. He was greatly influenced by his teacher, José Sabogal, the leader

Self-portrait by Camilo Blas

of a movement in Peruvian art known as indigenism. Indigenism refers to paintings showing Indians, the original inhabitants of Peru. This movement attracted a lot of attention because up until then most Peruvian artists painted European themes. Between 1925 and 1927, Blas studied the environment in Cuzco, located high in the Andes Mountains, with Sabogal. Blas learned a lot about the region and its people, who are mostly descendants of the Incas.

Apart from painting, Blas also taught at the National School of Fine Arts. He worked as a staff artist for the Archeological Museum in Lima. Blas died in 1985. He and the other indigenist painters will always be remembered in Peru for using the arts to show nationalism. Their paintings of Indians symbolized the pride of Peruvians in their native culture.

This painting is called *Paisaje serrano*, which means "mountain landscape." Blas loved to paint landscapes, especially the mountains, which showed the natural beauty of his country. This painting shows his attention to line and form. It also shows his use of harmonious colors and warm tones, which makes him stand out from other indigenist painters. His vision of the Indian in his geographical world was the main subject of this painting.

Blas painted *Paisaje serrano* in 1936. He used oil on canvas. The painting measures approximately 28 inches x 20 inches (70 cm x 50 cm). It is an example of indigenist art, in which Peru's indians are shown going about their daily lives.

Map of Peru

PERU

Map of the Continent of South America

Peru is on the west coast of South America. Ecuador and Colombia lie to the north, and Chile lies to the south. Brazil and Bolivia border Peru on the east, while the Pacific Ocean lies to the west. Peru is the third-largest country in South America, after Brazil and Argentina. Peru has three land regions. They are the coast, the Andes Mountains, and the jungle. The coast is a narrow desert along the Pacific Ocean. The Andes consist of two mountain ranges that run the length of Peru, separating the coast from the jungle. Huascarán is Peru's highest mountain at 22,205 feet (6,768 m). To the east of the Andes is the jungle. The Amazon River, which is the longest river in South America at 4,000 miles (6,437 km), flows through this region.

1

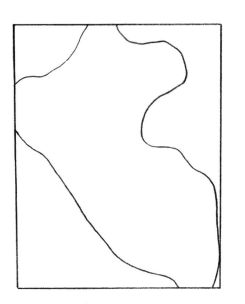

Begin by drawing a large rectangle. Carefully draw the wavy lines inside the rectangle. These will be your guides to drawing the map of Peru.

2

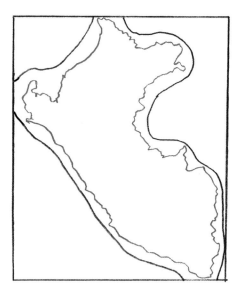

Inside of the guidelines you can draw the outline of the country Peru as shown.

3

Erase the guides and the rectangle. Well done, you have just drawn Peru!

4

☆	Lima (capital city)
∿	The Amazon River
⬫	Lake Titicaca
▣	Machu Picchu
◉	Colca Canyon

Finish your drawing by adding the symbols shown on the map key to mark some of Peru's areas of interest.

Flag of Peru

The flag of Peru has three vertical stripes. The middle stripe is white, and the side stripes are red. The national coat of arms is shown at the center of the white stripe. General José de San Martín of Argentina, who announced Peruvian independence in 1821, designed the Peruvian flag. He chose red and white as the flag's colors after seeing parihuanas in flight. The parihuana is a kind of flamingo that is red except for its white breast.

Currency of Peru

The currency in Peru is called *nuevo sol*, meaning "new sun" in Spanish. One nuevo sol equals 100 centimos. Peru's coins come in 1, 5, 10, 20, and 50 centimos. There is also a one–nuevo sol coin. The paper currency comes in values of 10, 20, 50, and 100 nuevo sols. Each bill shows the picture of an important person in Peru's history on its front and a scene showing Peruvian culture on its back.

Flag

1

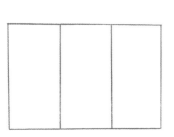

Draw a rectangle. Add two vertical lines in the rectangle as shown. You now have three bands that are equal in size.

2

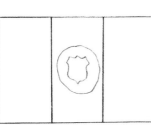

Draw a circle in the center band. In this circle draw the shape shown. This is the crest in Peru's coat of arms.

3

Between the circle and the crest, add the shapes shown.

4

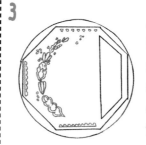

Add details as shown to the inside of the crest. Erase the guidelines. Finish your drawing by shading Peru's coat of arms and the two side bands.

Nuevo Sol

1

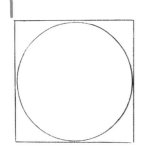

Begin by drawing a square. Draw a circle inside the square. The circle is the outer edge of the coin.

2

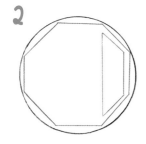

Erase the square. Draw an octagon inside the circle. An octagon is an eight-sided shape. On the right side of the octagon, draw a trapezoid that is on its side.

3

Add the details to the top, bottom, and left sides of the coin as shown. Add the shapes of flowers, in a curve, on the left side of the coin as shown.

4

Finish your drawing by adding the writing "UN NUEVO SOL" in the middle of the coin. You can add shading to the trapezoid as shown.

Peru's Coat of Arms

   General Simon Bolívar of Venezuela, who helped to free Peru from Spain, passed a law in 1825 to make Peru's coat of arms official.

   The coat of arms is divided into three parts. At the top left is a field of blue showing a vicuña, which is a very important animal in Peru because of its fine wool. At the top right is a field of white on which there is a cinchona tree, which is Peru's national tree. It is the source of quinine, an ingredient used to treat malaria. Malaria is a sickness that causes high fevers and chills and that is spread by a certain type of mosquito. Malaria is common in South America. Across the bottom of the national coat of arms is a field of red, which has a horn with golden coins flowing from it. The symbols in the national coat of arms represent Peru's richness in wildlife, plants, and mineral resources. Above the coat of arms is a green wreath framed by branches of palm and laurel. Peru's flag and national banner can be seen behind the coat of arms.

1

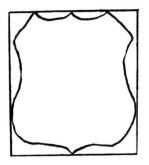

Start by drawing a rectangle. Draw the shape as shown on the inside of the rectangle. This is the beginning of the shield that appears in Peru's coat of arms.

2

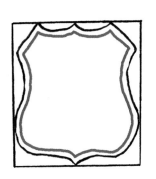

Draw another line, mirroring the shape you have just drawn, on the inside of the shield.

3

Erase the rectangle. Next draw a horizontal line across the center of the shield. Draw two more horizontal lines above the one you have just drawn. Leave a space between these lines as shown. Add two vertical lines that come from the middle edges of the horizontal lines. Erase the edges where the lines you have drawn meet the edge of the shield.

4

Add the shapes shown. In the top left corner draw the vicuña, the national animal in Peru. In the top right corner, draw Peru's national tree, the cinchona. In the bottom section, add the horn.

5

Add details to each of the symbols you have drawn.

6

You can finish your drawing with shading. Notice how the top right section of the crest remains white behind the tree. Well done! You did a great job.

The Kantuta

Peru's national flower is a tubelike blossom called the kantuta (*Cantua buxifolia*). The plant can grow up to 10 feet (3 m) high. It has stems and branches that bend. The leaves are small and gray-green, while the flowers are usually bright shades of pink or purple. There are also white and striped kantutas. The flower has many nicknames, one of which is the sacred flower of the Incas. It is native to Peru, Bolivia, and northern Chile.

The kantuta was very important to the Incas. They even named one of their districts the Kantuta or Flower District. This district was in their capital, Cuzco, which is located in the central highlands. The Kantuta also grows plentifully on Amantani Island, which is located in Lake Titicaca. The island is also known as the Island of the Kantuta.

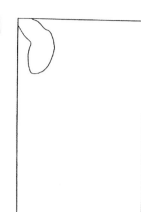

1

Start by drawing a rectangle. In the top left corner of the rectangle, add the shape shown.

4

Erase the rectangle and the guides. Add the squiggly lines to the bud at the top. Add the shapes to the top parts of the flowers. These are the buds from which the flowers have grown.

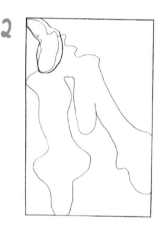

2

Draw the lines as shown inside the shape you just drew. This is a bud of the kantuta. Draw guide shapes for the rest of the flower. These will help you to position the flowers as they appear in the photograph.

5

Add more details to the top part of your drawing. Draw lines at the bottom of the flower parts to show where the lower petals, or parts of a flower, open.

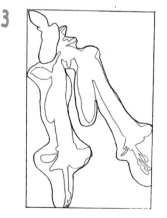

3

Erase the top guideline at the bud. In the shapes you just drew, add the wavy lines as shown. These are the flower parts of the kantuta. There are some leaves at the top.

6

Finish drawing the kantuta by adding shading as shown. Notice where the shading is darker in some parts than in others. Well done! You are finished.

The Cock of the Rocks

Peru's national bird is the cock of the rocks (*Rupicola peruviana*). It is native to the country. It lives in the forests high in the Andes Mountains. The cock can also be found in Bolivia.

The cock of the rocks has bright, shiny, orange-red feathers. It is about 1 foot (.3 m) in length and eats fruit. This bird is usually shy, so even with its bright color it cannot be spotted easily. However, when it is time for mating, the males gather on the treetops to display themselves to the females. The males flap their wings with force, jump around, and make noises.

Natives of the forests are known to eat the meat of the birds and to use their feathers for costumes. This may be one of the reasons that the cock of the rocks is an endangered species.

1

Begin by drawing a rough oval shape as shown. This will be a guide to drawing the top part of the cock of the rocks. Draw the shape inside the guide as shown.

2

Draw the outline of the bird's body, using the shape shown. Make sure you connect this shape to the shape you drew in step 2.

3

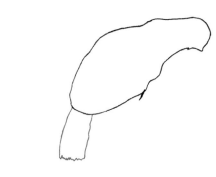

Erase the guideline at the top. At the bottom left-hand side of your drawing, add the bird's tail. Notice how the line at the bottom of the tail is slightly squiggly.

4

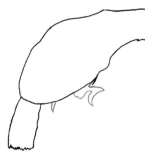

Draw a small pointed shape for the claw as shown. Beside it add another shape for the bird's foot with more claws showing.

5

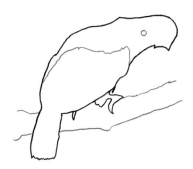

Add a circle for the eye. Draw a wavy line as shown across the bird's body. Add more lines for the branch of the tree on which the bird is sitting.

6

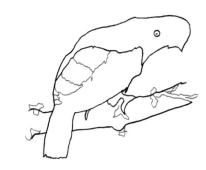

Add lines and shapes to the bird's body. These lines show some of the details of the bird's wings and feathers. Add a dot on the inside of the circle for the eye. Add details to the branch you drew in the last step.

7

Erase extra lines. Finish your drawing with shading. You can make the shading darker in some areas. For example, the bird's underbelly and tail can be dark, as can the leaves on the branch. Also, shade the branch, which will help to show the roughness of the wood.

The Vicuña

    The vicuña is the national animal of Peru and can be found in the Andes Mountains. It is the smallest member of the camel family, measuring a little more than 3 feet (1 m) high. Vicuñas have long necks and pointed ears. The color of their fur ranges from golden brown to red-brown. Centuries ago, the Incan rulers greatly valued vicuña wool. A few women were chosen to weave vicuña wool into clothes worn only by Incan rulers. The Incas would round up the vicuñas and clip their wool, but they always released them into the wild afterward. Vicuña wool is still valued today. Vicuñas had been hunted so much in recent years that they were in danger of disappearing. In 1964, they were considered an endangered species. To protect the vicuñas, the government created natural reserves where no hunting is allowed.

1

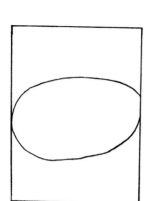

Start by drawing a rectangle. Draw an oval shape inside the rectangle. Your oval should not close on the right side. These shapes are your guides to drawing the vicuña.

2

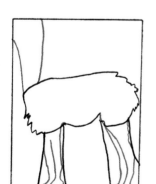

Draw the large shape for the body inside the oval as shown. From the shape you have just drawn, draw four lines. These will be your guides to drawing the vicuña's legs.

3

Erase the oval. Draw two lines extending from the top of the body. Next, fill in the legs in the guides you drew in step 3. Make sure you add the curved shapes for the feet.

4

Erase the leg guides. Erase the lines at the top of the legs where they meet the body, as shown. Outline the neck, head, and ears at the top of the drawing as shown.

5

Erase the guides. Erase the line where the neck meets the body. Add more details to the ears. Add the eyes, nose, and mouth. Draw a curved line at the front of the vicuña. Add lines under the belly and on the back legs to show fur.

6

Finish your drawing by adding lines for the fur and shading as shown.

Chavin de Huantar

The Chavin people created the first civilization in Peru between 900 and 200 B.C. They influenced other cultures through their beautiful designs in gold and silver, on cloths, and on ceramics. Their style of design spread throughout much of central and northern Peru. A religious center called Chavin de Huantar is the most important symbol of the Chavin culture. The center is located in the northeastern highlands of Peru. It is made of buildings, underground rooms, tunnels, and stone carvings. The stone carvings show figures of humanlike gods as well as snakes, birds, and gargoyles. Many were carved for decoration, such as those on the walls of temples.

1

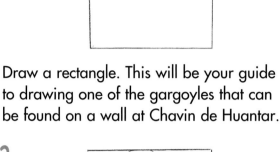

Draw a rectangle. This will be your guide to drawing one of the gargoyles that can be found on a wall at Chavin de Huantar.

2

Inside the rectangle draw the curved lines as shown. Notice how the lines at the top come into a slightly peaked shape.

3

Inside the guides you have just drawn, draw the outline of the gargoyle as shown. See how the top of the head comes into a peaked rounded shape.

4

Erase the rectangle and the guide. Toward the top of the head, draw a wavy line from left to right. Add the large wavy shape below it.

5

Draw circular shapes for the eyes, with a line coming out from each outer edge. Draw the nose and a line for the mouth. Add teeth that look like fangs, as shown.

6

Draw shapes inside the eyes. Add lines around the eye area. Add details to the forehead as shown. Draw more lines and shapes arond the nose and mouth areas.

7

Look at the photograph on the opposite page and add as much detail to your drawing as you like. You can finish your drawing of the gargoyle by adding shading. Notice where the shading is darker in some areas than in others. Good job!

27

Nazca Lines

In a desert near Nazca in southern Peru, there are mysterious giant drawings of lines, triangles, rectangles, animals, and other figures carved into  the sand. The animals include a spider, a monkey, a lizard, a pelican, and a hummingbird. The images are so big that they cannot be seen completely unless you are far above them, such as flying in an airplane. Maria Reiche was a German mathematician. She believed that the Nazca people, who lived around A.D. 500, carved the lines as a giant agricultural and religious calendar. She thought the lines were made to remind the gods about what the Nazca people needed. For example, the drawing of the monkey represented rain to the Nazca people. It was made during a drought, which is when there is no rain at all. The drawing was probably meant to remind the gods that the earth needed rain.

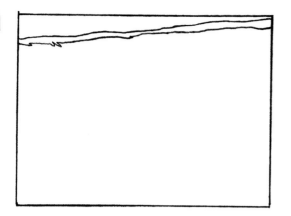

1

First look carefully at the photograph on the opposite page. Although the lines are faint, you can see the outline of a monkey with a long curly tail. Now start your picture by drawing a large rectangle. At the top of the rectangle, draw two rough lines that are close together, as shown.

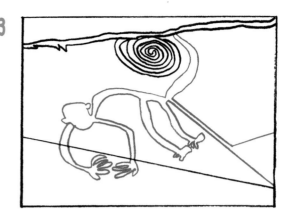

3

Now it is time to draw the monkey. Study the picture carefully and copy the shapes and outline of the monkey as best you can. Make sure you connect the tail to the top lines and that the monkey's arms cross over the bottom sloping line. Add extra sloping lines coming from the monkey's tail as shown.

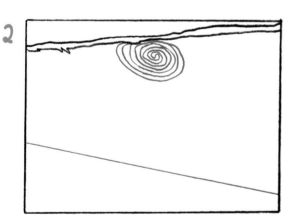

2

Draw two sets of lines that are in a curly shape at the top of your drawing as shown. This is the curly part of the monkey's tail. Draw a straight line across the bottom of the rectangle. Notice how it is angled slightly, sloping down from left to right.

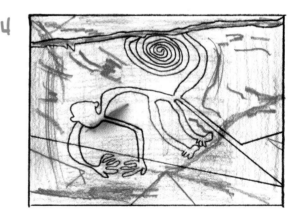

4

Add extra lines as shown. Finish your drawing by shading. Use your pencil to add thicker lines all over your drawing. Well done! You have just drawn the monkey that appears on the sand in the desert near Nazca, in the south of Peru.

Chan Chan

The Chimu kingdom in Peru existed from the early thirteenth century to the mid-fifteenth century. The Chimu capital was called Chan Chan, meaning "sun sun," and was located on the northern coast. It was made of nine compounds, or groups of buildings. All the buildings were made of adobe bricks. Adobe is sun-dried mud. Chan Chan was preserved for a long time because it is located in a very dry part of Peru. However, in 1925, it rained continuously for seven days in Chan Chan. The buildings melted into mounds of mud, and only the ruins remain today. These ruins include the remains of temples, palaces, houses, gardens, and streets. The sacred places in Chan Chan were surrounded by adobe walls.

1

Start your drawing with a rectangle. Draw a horizontal line across the top as shown.

2

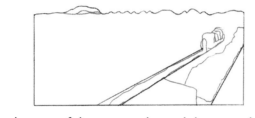

Draw a wavy line going across the horizontal line you just drew. Next, add three angled lines coming from the bottom of the rectangle as shown. These lines slope from the bottom left toward the top right side of the rectangle.

3

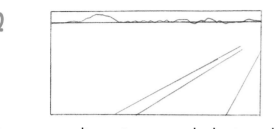

Erase the top of the rectangle and the straight horizontal line you drew in step 1. Add a wavy line under the curved shape at the top. Using the upward angled lines as guides, draw lines in and around them as shown.

4

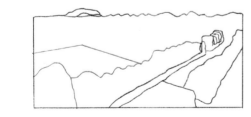

Erase the angled lines. In the bottom left corner of your drawing, draw a curved shape as shown. Draw a wavy line that extends from this shape to connect with one of the shapes you drew in step 3. On the left side of the drawing, draw two straight lines that meet at an angle as shown.

5

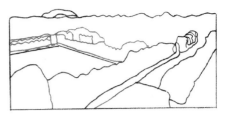

Add more lines and details as shown. All these shapes are the remains of the walls and buildings in Chan Chan.

6

Add more lines and shapes in the background as shown. Start at the top and work carefully as you draw the lines.

7

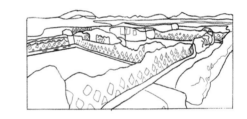

Now add some details to the walls and buildings in your drawing. Add lots of little diamonds and other rough shapes to the walls as shown. Add some squiggly lines to the rocks at the bottom right of the drawing. Draw some shapes in the building in the middle of the drawing as shown. Add lines to the top right side and at the front of the drawing.

8

Add details to the tops of the walls as shown. You can finish by shading. Be sure to shade the holes in the walls.

31

Machu Picchu

Machu Picchu is the best-preserved Incan city. Historians believe that it was built around 1420, when the Incan leader Pachacuti ruled Peru. Machu Picchu means "old mountain" in Quechuan. It was unknown to the outside world for many centuries because it was hard to reach. Located near the Incan capital of Cuzco, it lies on the edge of the Urubamba Canyon. Machu Picchu could be reached only by an Incan trail about 25 miles (40 km) long. The trail includes steps, stone paths, and tunnels crossing the Urubamba River. Machu Picchu's remains include temples, houses, and cemeteries, or places where the dead are buried.

Machu Picchu is surrounded by terraces that are carved into the mountainsides. The Incas used the terraces for farming.

1

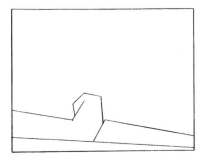

Draw a rectangle. Then draw a line that slopes from the bottom left of the rectangle to the bottom right. Add lines above this line as shown.

2

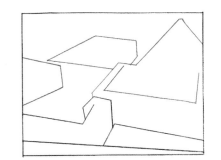

Look at the drawing carefully and add the various shapes shown. Work from left to right.

3

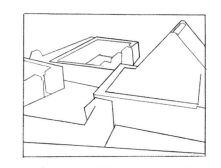

Add more lines and shapes in and around the shapes you drew in step 2. These are some of the buildings that are found in Machu Picchu.

4

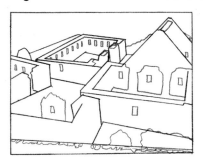

Looking carefully at the photograph on the opposite page, add the details of the windows and broken buildings as shown. Add the details to the walls and to the back of the main building as shown.

5

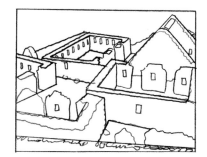

Erase the extra line at the bottom right of the drawing. Follow the straight guides around the buildings and draw a squiggly outline as shown. Add extra lines and shapes as shown.

6

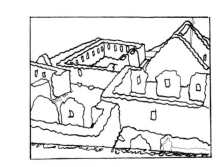

Erase extra lines. Add extra details, such as little shapes for rocks on the left, a vertical shape on the roof to the right, and some more lines at the front and back of the drawing as shown.

7

Add lines for the brick details throughout. You can finish your drawing with shading. Notice where the shading is darker in some parts than in others. Well done! You have finished drawing some of the remains at Machu Picchu.

33

Francisco Pizarro

Francisco Pizarro (1478–1541) led 180 Spaniards to conquer Peru in 1532. It was Pizarro's victory over the Incas, who ruled Peru at the time, that began 300 years of Spanish control of the country. He also brought the Roman Catholic religion to Peru. In the late 1530s, Pizarro quarreled with another Spaniard, Diego de Almagro, who had come to Peru with Pizarro. The two men fought over who should rule the area around Cuzco, the ancient capital of the Incas. This led to a war that Pizarro won, and Almagro was put to death in 1538. However, in 1541, Almagro's son and his followers killed Pizarro. The mummy of Pizarro is encased in a tomb in Lima Cathedral. Pizarro founded the city of Lima in 1535.

CAPITAN GENERAL
DON FRANCISCO PIZARRO

1

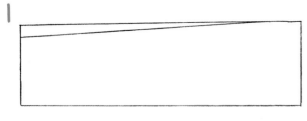

Begin by drawing a long rectangle. Add a line that slopes from the left side to the right. Start this line a little below the top of the rectangle and finish it before it reaches the end of the line at the top of the rectangle.

2

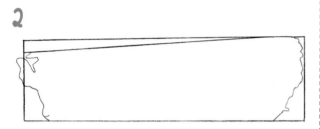

Draw some wavy lines on the left side of the drawing. Notice how these lines go outside the side of the rectangle. Draw another wavy line on the right side of the rectangle. These lines you have just drawn are the outline of the box in which the mummy of Pizarro lies.

3

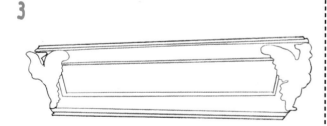

Erase most of the rectangular guide as shown. Add details to the shapes at the sides of the coffin as shown. Next add horizonal lines, drawn in pairs. In the middle section, add more lines at the sides that connect with the horizontal lines on each side.

4

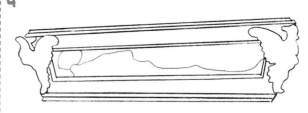

In the middle section, draw the outline of Pizarro's mummy. Draw a shape for the part of the head that is showing. Beside this, the arm's shape slopes upward. The line for the body then slopes down to the end where the outline of the foot is.

5

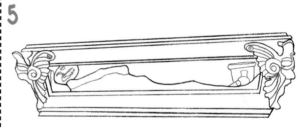

Add the details as shown to the decorations at each end of the coffin. Add lines and shapes to the mummy's head, or skull, and body. Add a small line to complete the headrest where the skull is placed. Add the shapes at the foot of the mummy.

6

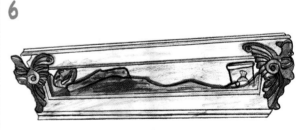

You can finish your drawing by shading the areas shown. Notice how dark the shading is on the upper part of the mummy and on the decorations at the sides of the coffin.

35

Convento de Santa Catalina

Arequipa, a city in southwestern Peru, is famous for its beautiful Spanish buildings and churches. Some of the most beautiful buildings in Arequipa can be found in the Convento de Santa Catalina. The convent is like a small town because it has a square, a church, and many buildings, streets, and gardens. For centuries Roman Catholic nuns lived in complete seclusion in the convent. As many as 1,000 nuns lived in the convent during the first half of the eighteenth century. The nuns were not allowed to go outside or even to show themselves to the people outside. It was not until 1970 that visitors were allowed inside the convent. Today there are fewer nuns in the convent. They live in parts of the convent where tourists are not allowed.

1

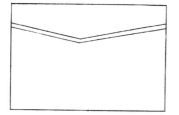

Start by drawing a rectangle. Add two sets of lines that slope and meet near the center as shown.

2

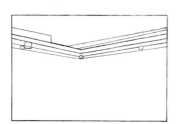

Add two more sets of lines under the lines you drew in step 1. Add three small circles between these lines as shown. Beside the circle on the left, add a shape that crosses the line. Add more sloping lines and a box shape along the top as shown.

3

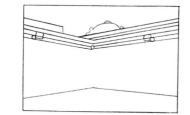

Draw the outline of a dome at the top of your drawing. Notice how there is a squiggly part on the left, and a small shape beside the curve of the dome on the right. Add another shape beside the circle on the right. Add more lines at the bottom of the drawing as shown.

4

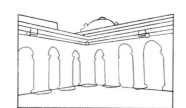

Erase the top of the rectangle guide. Draw the curved shapes as shown. These are arches and columns.

5

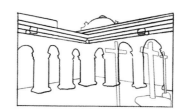

Erase the extra lines at the bottom of the columns. Add three cross shapes. See how the middle cross stands on a curved shape. The cross on the right stands on a smaller platform.

6

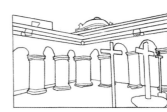

Erase the extra lines inside the crosses. Add the curved lines to the columns as shown. Add extra lines at the base of the columns as shown. Add lines beside the columns. Add details to the dome and to the roof on the left.

7

Add curved lines at the top of the archways. Add another curved line on the inside of the base of the middle cross. Add lines between the curved lines at the base of the middle cross. Add details to the roof area.

8

Add details to the columns and to the ground. Finish with shading. You can make the crosses and the areas between the columns darker. Some parts of the roof can be darker, too.

37

Cathedral of Cuzco

The Incas built their capital high in the Andes Mountains around A.D. 1100. They called it Cuzco, meaning "navel," or belly button, because the city formed the center of the Incan Empire.

When the Spanish took over Peru, they built many churches and buildings. They used local building supplies and the help of Indians. The resulting buildings reflect a mix of Indian and Spanish architectural styles. The Cathedral of Cuzco is one of the most beautiful examples of this mixed style. The cathedral is located in the same spot where an Incan palace used to stand. The building of the cathedral began in 1560 using stones from the palace. The finished cathedral measures 282 feet (86 m) by 150 feet (46 m). The cathedral contains many objects of great value, including a solid silver altar and 372 paintings.

1

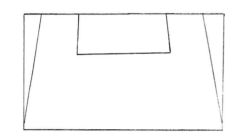

Draw a rectangle. Draw two angled lines at the sides of the rectangle as shown. Add two vertical lines and a horizontal line that form a rectangular shape at the top of your guide rectangle. You now have two towers.

2

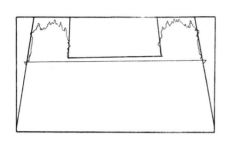

Draw a long horizontal line just underneath the towers. See how this line wraps around the angled lines at the side. Add squiggly lines to the towers as shown.

3

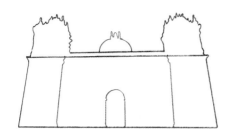

Erase the guidelines. Add two vertical lines that curve slightly at the ends as shown. Draw an arch shape for a door. Draw a dome shape, with squiggly lines at the top.

4

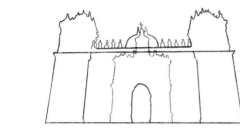

Add details to the front of the building and to the roof. Add the cross to the top of the dome.

5

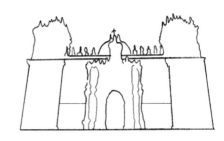

Erase extra lines. Add two vertical shapes in the door area as shown. Draw two short horizontal lines.

6

Add details around the arched doorway as shown. Next add curved lines over the horizontal lines you drew in step 5. Add small arches and windows.

7

Add details to the tops of the towers as shown. Add a circle for a clock to the left tower. Draw a series of horizontal lines as shown across the front of the building. Add two more doors and a window as shown.

You can add as much detail to the towers and doors as you like. You can finish your drawing with shading.

José de San Martín

José de San Martín (1778–1850) is a great hero. He helped Peru and other countries to become independent from Spain. He was born in Paso de los Libres, Argentina, to Spanish parents. When he was seven or eight years old, his family returned to Spain. San Martín

served as an army officer in Spain for 22 years. He left the army to join the patriots of Argentina in rebelling against Spain. He disliked the way Spain was treating the people in its colonies. He went on to help fight for the independence of Chile in 1818. In 1820, he led an army of Argentines and Chileans to attack the Spaniards in Peru. San Martín created a constitution that gave freedom to slaves and announced that the descendants of the Incas were citizens of Peru. Peruvians have built statues and named places in honor of San Martín. One such place is the Plaza de San Martín in Lima.

1

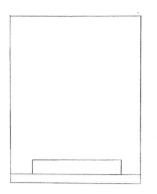

Begin by drawing a large rectangle. Draw a horizontal line at the bottom of the rectangle. Draw a rectangular shape on top of the horizontal line.

5

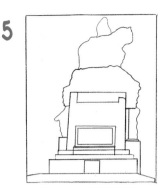

Draw two curved shapes at the top of your drawing. These are guides for drawing the horse and rider. Add squiggly lines on either side of the drawing as shown.

2

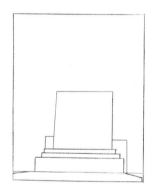

Draw two more rectangular shapes on top of the one you just drew. Notice how they get smaller in size. Draw the lines underneath the horizontal line.

6

Draw the horse and the rider inside your guidelines. Add details to the rest of the drawing as shown. Erase any extra lines.

3

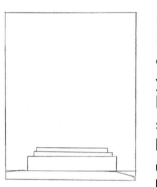

The rectangles you have drawn form a step shape. On top of this shape, draw lines to form a large rectangular shape and two smaller shapes at the sides.

7

Erase the guide rectangle. Erase the horse and rider guidelines. Look carefully at the photograph and add as much detail to the drawing as you like. Finish with shading. Great job!

4

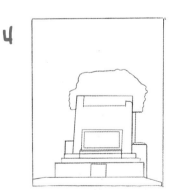

Add lines inside the shapes you have drawn. Draw more straight lines on the right side. Draw a rough curved line around the top of your drawing. Erase extra lines.

Lake Titicaca and the Floating Islands

   Lake Titicaca is South America's second-largest lake, after Lake Maracaibo in Venezuela. Half of Lake Titicaca is in Peru and the other half is in Bolivia. It is about 350 miles (563 km) in length and 100 miles (161 km) in width. It is located at an elevation of 12,500 feet (3,810 m) above sea level, making it the world's highest body of water that is deep and wide enough for boats to sail on.

   In the middle of Lake Titicaca are floating islands made of piles of tall grasses called reeds. A group of Indians known as the Uros live on these islands. They live as their descendants lived hundreds of years ago, by fishing, hunting birds, and gathering lake plants that are good to eat.

1

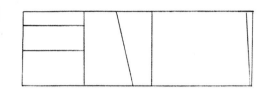

Draw a rectangle. Add two vertical lines inside the rectangle as shown. You now have three sections in the rectangle. In the left section, draw two horizontal lines. In the middle and right sections, draw sloping lines as shown.

2

In the left section, draw the shapes below the horizontal lines as shown. Draw the shape in the middle section, making sure you connect the bottom line to the line in the first section. Add the lines to the last section as shown.

3

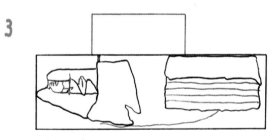

Erase the guidelines. Add two vertical lines and one horizontal line at the top of your drawing as shown. Add lines and shapes to the rest of the drawing as shown.

4

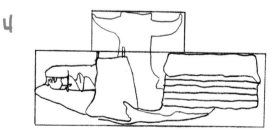

In the top rectangle, draw the shape shown. Extend this shape to the middle part of the drawing. Add the thin vertical shape on the left. Add a wavy line at the bottom.

5

Erase both rectangles. Look carefully at the photograph and this drawing of the floating islands, and copy the lines and shapes as shown. Notice the three shapes in the middle part of the drawing. These are windows in one of the houses on the island.

6

Add more lines to the top of the middle structure as shown. Add a ladder coming from this structure as shown. Draw more lines and a squiggly line at the bottom as shown.

7

Add thin lines to the houses and the boat on the island as shown. This will give the effect of the reeds from which the houses are made. Finish with shading. Well done! You did a super job.

43

Timeline

20,000 B.C.	People from Asia spread throughout the Americas and arrive in Peru.
900 B.C.	The Chavin civilization develops in Peru.
500	The Nazca civilization develops on the south coast of Peru. At about the same time, the Moche civilization grows in the north.
1200	The start of the Chimu kingdom.
1450	The Incas invade the Chimu people and take over their kingdom.
1463–1493	The Incas expand their territory.
1532	Francisco Pizarro and a group of Spaniards arrive on Peru's northern coast.
1535	Pizarro founds the city of Lima.
1541	Pizarro is killed by the son of his Spanish rival.
1800s	Other Spanish colonies in South America rebel.
1820s	Disagreement between Peru and Ecuador over the border they share begins.
1821	General José de San Martín of Argentina announces Peru's independence from Spain.
1823	General Simon Bolívar of Venezuela leads the attack against Spaniards in Peru to complete the country's separation from Spain.
1826	Bolívar's soldiers finally defeat the Spanish in Peru.
1827	General José de la Mar is elected the first Peruvian president.
1941	Peru and Ecuador go to war over a disagreement about their common border.
1980	The Peruvian military agrees to democratic civilian elections.
1993	Peru creates a new constitution, under which the people elect a president to a five-year term.

Peru Fact List

Official Name	Republica del Peru (Republic of Peru)
Area	496,255 square miles (1,285,294 sq km)
Population	26,500,000
Capital	Lima, population, 6,000,000
Most-Populated City	Lima
Industries	Chemicals, furniture, paper products, steel, textiles
Agriculture	Coffee, cotton, sugarcane, potatoes, bananas
National Flower	Kantuta
National Tree	Cinchona (or quinine tree)
National Bird	Gallito de las rocas (cock of the rocks)
National Dance	Marinera
National Anthem	"We Are Free, Let Us Always Be So"
Languages	Spanish and Quechuan
Highest Mountain Peak	Huascarán, 22,205 feet (6,768 m)
Longest River	Amazon River, 4,000 miles (6,437 km)
National Holidays	New Year's Day, January 1; Independence Day, July 28–29; Saint Rose of Lima Day, August 30

Glossary

ancestry (AN-ses-tree) Having to do with relatives who lived long ago.

architectural (ar-kih-TEK-chuh-rul) Having to do with the style and the creation of buildings.

Bering Land Bridge (BAYR-ing LAND BRIJ) The strip of land that once formed a means of crossing from Siberia to Alaska, where the Bering Strait is today.

cathedral (kuh-THEE-drul) A Large church that is run by bishops.

Catholic (KATH-lik) Someone who belongs to the Roman Catholic faith.

ceramics (suh-RA-miks) Things that are made from matter, such as clay, that are heated until they harden.

chemicals (KEH-mih-kulz) Matter that can be mixed with other matter to cause changes.

constitution (kon-stih-TOO-shun) The basic rules by which a country is governed.

convent (KON-vent) A place where nuns live.

convento (kon-VEN-toh) A Spanish word for a place where members of a religious order live.

culture (KUL-chur) The beliefs, practices, and arts of a group of people.

descendants (dih-SEN-dents) People who are born of a certain family or group.

designed (dih-ZYND) Planned or formed something.

develop (dih-VEH-lup) To grow.

dialects (DY-uh-lekt) Kinds of languages spoken only in a certain area.

drought (DROWT) A period of dryness that causes harm to crops.

elevation (eh-luh-VAY-shun) The height of an object.

endangered species (en-DAYN-jerd SPEE-sheez) Describing an animal whose species or group have almost all died out.

executed (EK-suh-kyoot-ed) Put to death.

expanded (ek-SPAND-ed) Spread out, or grew larger.

fertilizer (FUR-til-eye-zer) A substance put in soil to help crops grow.

gargoyles (GAR-goylz) Carved, animal-like figures with scary faces.

historians (hih-STOR-ee-unz) People who study the past.

independence (in-dih-PEN-dents) Freedom from the control or support of others.

influenced (IN-floo-ensd) To have swayed others without using force.

inhabited (in-HA-bit-ed) Occupied as a place of residence.

introduced (in-truh-DOOSD) To have brought into use, knowledge, or notice.

invade (in-VAYD) To enter a place in order to attack and take over.

mathematician (math-muh-TIH-shun) A person who studies numbers.

mineral (MIH-ner-ul) A natural element that is not an animal or a plant.

nomads (NOH-madz) People who move from place to place.

official (uh-FIH-shul) Having proof that something is formal or legal.

parallel (PAR-uh-lel) Being side by side.

patriots (PAY-tree-uts) People who love and defend their country.

reeds (REEDZ) Tall, slender pieces of grass.

resources (REE-sors-ez) Supplies or sources of energy or useful items.

ruins (ROO-enz) Old, falling-down buildings.

sacred (SAY-kred) Blessed by the church; highly respected and important.

seclusion (seh-KLOO-zhen) The state of being kept away from other people.

South America (SOWTH uh-MER-ih-kuh) A continent that includes the countries of Argentina, Bolivia, Brazil, Chile, Colombia, Ecuador, Paraguay, Peru, Uruguay, and Venezuela.

symbolized (SIM-buh-lyz) To have stood for something.

terraces (TER-us-ez) Raised parts of land with a flat top and sloping sides.

territory (TER-uh-tor-ee) Land that is controlled by a person or a group of people.

textiles (TEK-stylz) Woven fabrics or cloth.

tomb (TOOM) A grave.

tourists (TUR-ists) People who take a trip or a tour for pleasure.

trail (TRAYL) A path or track made from repeated passage or made on purpose.

Index

Web Sites

Due to the changing nature of Internet links, PowerKids Press has developed an online list of Web sites related to the subject of this book. This site is updated regularly. Please use this link to access the list:
www.powerkidslinks.com/kgdc/peru/